SAINT MADELEINE SOPHIE
BARAT
(1779 – 1865)

FOUNDER OF THE
SOCIETY OF THE SACRED HEART OF JESUS

Frances Gimber, RSCJ

Saint Madeleine Sophie Barat (1779-1865)
Founder of the Society of the Sacred Heart of Jesus

Copyright © 2024 Society of the Sacred Heart. All rights reserved. No part of this book may be used or reproduced by any means, graphic, electronic, or mechanical, including photocopying, recording, taping or by any information storage retrieval system without the written permission of the editor except in the case of brief quotations embodied in articles and reviews.

Cover illustration: Painting by Savinien Petit, 1870
Book design by Peggy Nehmen, n-kcreative.com

Printed in the United States of America
ISBN-13: 978-1-7364924-3-7 (paperback) ♦ 978-1-7364924-4-4 (ebook)

Published by:

 Society of the Sacred Heart™
United States – Canada

4120 Forest Park Avenue
St. Louis Missouri 63108-2809
314-652-1500
www.rscj.org

 @RSCJUSC
facebook.com/SocietyoftheSacredHeart
facebook.com/ReligiousOfTheSacredHeart
(Vocations)

CONTENTS

Introduction v
1. Beginnings 1
2. Revolution 5
3. Vocation 9
4. Becoming Religious 13
5. The Society Forms 17
6. Divergence 23
7. A New Start 27
8. Growth in France 29
9. Further Expansion 33
10. Papal Approbation 37
11. Political Troubles 41
12. Italy and Further Expansion 45
13. Crisis 49
14. Expansion: New Lands 53
15. Internal Challenge 57
16. Further Revolutions 59
17. Consolidation 61
18. Old Age 65
19. Last acts of governance 69
Afterword 71
Chronology 75

INTRODUCTION

WHO IS MADELEINE SOPHIE BARAT? She was a nineteenth century French nun who founded a congregation of sisters who have worked as educators at first in France and subsequently in all five continents. The Roman Catholic Church canonized her, that is, declared her a saint, in 1925, much to the joy of the sisters of her congregation and their alumnae. Canonization is a lengthy, expensive process involving collecting testimonies about the life of the persons concerned and doing research into their writings. In Madeleine Sophie's case, those writings consisted of 14,000 letters. Several scholars have written biographies, and some are still studying those letters. This brief work is an attempt to see what it was about her that motivated surviving religious and clergy to go to the trouble and expense of the canonization process and to continue to study her life and her thinking. What is the significance of her life and achievement for us in the twenty-first century, so far removed from the social and cultural conditions of her times?

—Frances Gimber, RSCJ

Barat Family Home

1

BEGINNINGS

MADELEINE SOPHIE BARAT came from the town of Joigny in Burgundy, on the edge of Champagne in wine country. In November 1779, a fire broke out in the town that threatened the houses along the rue du Puits Chardon (now rue Davier).

One house, 11 rue Davier, still shows the marks of that fire. The family of a vine grower and barrel maker named Jacques Barat lived in that house. His wife, Marie-Madeleine Fouffé, who was expecting her third child, was so traumatized by dread of the fire that she gave birth two months early. Her baby girl was born during the night of December 12-13. As the child was quite frail, she was hurried to the Church of Saint Thibaut across the street early the next morning to be baptized, her eleven-year-old brother Louis standing as godfather. As godmother, a woman of the parish who had come for morning Mass was chosen. Little Madeleine Sophie, as she was christened, survived, to the joy of her parents, her brother and older sister Marie-Louise. She was precocious; she knew her catechism so well by the age of ten that she was judged ready to make her first Communion at that early age. She

2 | Saint Madeleine Sophie Barat

Baptismal font where Sophie was baptized.

was a happy little girl, maybe somewhat spoiled, as she was the joy of her parents. She did not go to school, except for the catechism classes in the parish. She seems to have acquired practical knowledge because it is told that as an adolescent, accompanying

Sophie as a young girl

her mother to an appointment on a financial matter, she was able to explain a complicated issue more clearly than her mother could.

As for her brother Louis, eleven years older, he was a serious boy with ambition to be a priest; he did go to school to the minor seminary in the town, École Saint-Jacques. Studies there were followed by some years in a major seminary and ordination as a deacon. He then took up teaching at his old school while waiting to be old enough for ordination to the priesthood. In the meantime, he undertook Sophie's education. Whether he realized that her native intelligence needed developing or believed that his role in her life as godfather gave him some responsibility for her education, he insisted on a rather strict program of study and religious practice for a little girl. She followed more or less the program of study in use with the boys in the minor seminary; it included classical and modern languages and mathematics. The result was that she was educated well beyond the norm for girls of her class and era. This education she would not have received, had it not been for Louis; it would play a significant part in her future.

2

REVOLUTION

AS SOPHIE WAS GROWING UP, political turmoil was deepening in France. She was almost ten years old when the storming of the Bastille took place in Paris, on July 14, 1789, thus launching the violent aspect of the French Revolution. The National Assembly, which had been inaugurated that year, soon passed an edict requiring priests to take an oath pledging loyalty to the state through the Civil Constitution of the Clergy, a structure that placed the clergy in the employ of the state rather than the Church. Louis, a deacon, followed the example of his archbishop and took the oath. In 1790, the pope condemned the Civil Constitution and excommunicated priests who took it. Louis thereupon recanted publicly, exposing himself to arrest. For a time he hid in the attic of the family home; but when he was discovered, he escaped to Paris to avoid punishment. He was recognized there, however, and imprisoned. For a time, his family's goods were sequestered as a consequence of his law-breaking. Louis escaped the guillotine through the kindness of a former pupil who was in a position to prevent his name from appearing on the list of those to be executed. Released from prison after the fall of Robespierre in 1794, Louis remained in Paris. Sometime during those months, he was ordained a priest secretly, as religious worship was still forbidden.

Before his imprisonment, he had found engravings of the Hearts of Jesus and Mary in a shop and sent them home to Joigny, where his mother had them framed and hung in the house; the family prayed before them each night. Mme Barat took a risk in displaying these images because the Sacred Heart was a symbol used by the Catholic opponents of the Revolution. Besides, the region around Joigny was heavily influenced by Jansenism, a spiritual movement that emphasized the sinfulness of human beings and the judgment of God. Jansenists disapproved of the symbol of the Sacred Heart with its emphasis on God's love and mercy. Mme Barat and her family were Jansenists, so it is all the more surprising that she allowed these images. Her love for Louis and anxiety about him caused her to cherish them as gifts from him.

During these tense weeks, Mme Barat was deeply troubled about her son and about conditions in Joigny. Under the Civil Constitution, at first, the priests who had taken the oath continued to celebrate Mass and the ordinary sacraments in the parishes; but as the excesses of the Revolution multiplied, churches were closed and Catholic worship forbidden. In Joigny, all three churches, including Saint-Thibaut, were either closed or given over to revolutionary celebrations like worship of the goddess of Reason.

Sophie not only shared in the anxiety but felt the responsibility of caring for her mother. There was a time, for example, when her mother would not eat. The only way Sophie could get her to eat was to refuse to eat herself. Sophie prepared a dish her mother

Embroidery

especially liked; when she set it before her and her mother refused it, Sophie said she would not eat either. That changed her mother's mind. For Sophie these years of her adolescence were fraught with stress, conflict and uncertainty. Both church and family were in disarray. In Louis's absence, her study was interrupted. She seems to have spent her time doing needlework; on a civic document her occupation is listed as a seamstress. If the embroidery of the two hearts of Jesus and Mary attributed to her is indeed her work, she was an extremely skilled needlewoman.

    When conditions improved politically and the danger had subsided, Louis came home, an ordained priest by then. He intended to go back to Paris, however, to seek some form of ministry; and he proposed that Sophie accompany him, as he believed there would be opportunities for her development that Joigny did not offer and that he could continue her education. She had aspirations to the life of a Carmelite nun, although the life had not yet been revived in France. If a convent were to reopen, it would no doubt be in Paris. There would also be opportunities for apostolic work among children, as schools were one of the casualties of the Revolution. Jacques Barat approved of his daughter's going; his approval combined with Louis's insistence overcame Mme Barat's opposition. It was decided that Sophie would go to Paris on condition that she would return every year at the time of the grape harvest, a season of celebration as well as of hard work.

3

VOCATION

IN PARIS LOUIS FOUND lodgings for Sophie with a widow, Mme Duval, in the rue de Touraine in the Marais in the center of Paris on the right bank of the Seine. Sophie was joined by a young woman whom Louis was directing, Octavie Bailly, and Marguerite, Mme Duval's maid, whose surname we do not know. A single woman, Marie-Françoise Loquet, a catechism teacher and writer, joined the little community by day for spiritual exercises, especially talks by Louis, and serious study of Scripture, the writings of the Fathers of the Church, and classical authors. They lived an austere life of silence, prayer and penance including fasting and little sleep under Louis's guidance. The severity of the regime was to have repercussions on Sophie's health in the future; Louis did not take into consideration the physical needs of a young woman. At the same time, his strictness had harmful effects on her sensitive conscience. All her life she would tend to see herself as sinful. It was only later spiritual directors who would help her to overcome her self-deprecation. Reminiscing about those days later, Sophie would tell her hearers that sometimes she protected herself by just laughing at her brother's demands. Once when he told her she would never be a saint, she retorted, "Then I shall compensate by being very humble." She kept that resolution, and when the Church canonized her, it would be for her humility.

Louis, in the meantime, had joined a group of priests called the Fathers of the Faith. They were a branch of a Roman society of priests that was just getting started in France under Father Joseph Varin, who was charged also with establishing a branch of a female society associated with the Fathers of the Faith called the *Dilette di Gesù* (Beloved of Jesus).

Before Joseph Varin joined the Fathers of the Faith, he had been a seminarian in Paris; his seminary was closed at the outbreak of the Revolution, and many of the young men went abroad. Varin joined a small group who had particular devotion to the Sacred Heart of Jesus. Once they were ordained, they called themselves the Society of the Sacred Heart; they lived a strict religious life together, even thought of becoming Trappists or, still more, Jesuits. The Society of Jesus had been suppressed by Pope Clement XIV in most of Europe in 1773, but these men hoped it would soon be restored in France, and they could join it. The moving spirit of this group was one Léonor de Tournély (1767-1797). He realized that the restoration of Christian family life in France would require not only dedicated priests but also women who were educated in their faith. To this end, he had seen the need of a congregation of women religious who would undertake the education of girls. He saw dedication to the Heart of Jesus as the spiritual basis of the proposed society. Father de Tournély died at the age of twenty-nine before seeing the realization of his hope for the women's group, but he confided his dream to Joseph Varin. When Varin later joined the Fathers of the Faith and was sent to establish that society in France, he had in mind also the mission confided to him by Léonor de Tournély. He saw in the *Dilette di Gesú* the possible realization of de Tournély's dream. Father Varin, therefore, was looking for some French women to establish the *Dilette* in France.

When he heard of Louis's sister, he asked to meet her. She was at home in Joigny at the time; but when she returned, she was introduced to Father Varin, who thought that the advanced education she had received from Louis meant that she was suited to join the *Dilette*, whose work was to be educating young women. At Sophie's protest that she wanted to be a Carmelite, he replied that her superior education should not be buried in the cloister but put at the service of other young women. Father Varin soon joined Louis Barat in directing the small community in the rue de Touraine. He arranged for them to consecrate themselves to the Sacred Heart of Jesus at a ceremony on November 21, 1800, feast of the Presentation of Mary in the Temple of Jerusalem. This ceremony, held in the chapel in the apartment where they were living, would in the future be identified as the founding moment of the Society of the Sacred Heart, although the participants, Sophie included, made the consecration that day as members of the *Dilette di Gesù*.

Now it was necessary to look for an opportunity for them to exercise an educational ministry. Varin learned about a small boarding school in Amiens being run by a former Benedictine nun, Hyacinthe Devaux, who was looking for assistants or even for someone to whom she could hand over the work. She had a niece, Henriette Grosier, who was searching for religious life; her friend, Geneviève Deshayes, was interested also. Father Varin, seeing the opportunity he was looking for, put all these people in

L'Oratoire, still today a Sacred Heart school.

touch with one another. The result was that Sophie and her companions from Paris went to Amiens and, joined by Genevieve and Henriette, in January 1801, started the first school of the Society of the Sacred Heart. There were several changes of location in the city, but they ended up in a former religious house called *l'Oratoire*, still today a Sacred Heart school.

These women were for the most part inexperienced in education; but fortunately among the Fathers of the Faith, who had already established a school for boys, there were some trained educators who helped the women consistently with curriculum and teaching methods. One of these, Nicolas Loriquet, who later became a Jesuit, remained a trusted advisor to Sophie in educational matters. Boarders continued to enroll, and before long, the sisters were able to establish classes in practical subjects for poor girls and women.

4

BECOMING RELIGIOUS

THE GROUP PREPARED to establish themselves as religious, and on November 21, 1801, the anniversary of the first consecration in Paris, Sophie and Genevieve Deshayes and Henriette Grosier made the official three vows of religion as members of the *Dilette di Gesù*. At first, Mademoiselle Loquet, as the older and more experienced among them, was named to head the group. Her leadership was questionable; she herself had no experience of religious life, and, though she had been involved in religious education, she had never run a school. Some other women soon joined them, and one in particular saw the problems with Mlle Loquet and alerted Father Varin. Soon, in August 1802, one of the senior members of the *Dilette*, Louise Naudet, came from Rome to visit and assess the situation. She decided that the one who had the capacity to lead the group was the youngest, Sophie Barat. Early in her visit, finding Sophie too shy, she said to her, "You really must come out of yourself." Sophie asked—to everyone's amusement—"May I never go in again?" She was not so much shy as drawn to the interior life of prayer and solitude. There is a tradition in the

Society that at a later meeting of the community with Father Varin, he asked Sophie the catechism question: "Why did God make you"? Her answer, of course, was something like, "To do his will, Father." To which Father Varin rejoined, "And his will is that you should be superior." She was devastated at first, feeling no ability whatsoever to fulfill the task, but she had the confidence of the group and accepted out of obedience. It was not only Louise Naudet who recognized Sophie's capacity for leadership; her older companions also supported the choice. She was to hold the office of superior until her death sixty-three years later.

Mlle Loquet soon withdrew, seeing the group as leaderless without herself: "I really don't know what will become of this house. Sister Grosier can't even sweep her room; Sister Deshayes just trots around, and Sister Sophie can't put two words together." Octavie Bailly was sent to Rome to learn from the *Dilette* how to be a director of novices, as the plan was that she would take on that responsibility in Amiens. When she returned to France after the later separation from the *Dilette*, however, she decided to enter the Carmelites. In the end, therefore, of those who started out Sophie was alone with Marguerite. She missed Octavie with whom she had become a close friend.

Others soon came to join the community; there were many former religious in France whose convents had been closed during the Revolution. As a result of the Concordat of 1801, the agreement between the Vatican and the government of Napoleon, many of them saw that religious life would be possible again and were looking to live it once more. One of these, Anne Baudemont, who had been a Poor Clare of a branch that had run a boarding school in Rheims, joined the group in Amiens. Her educational and religious experience was viewed as an advantage. An interesting family came along also, the de Gramonts, a mother and two daughters of the aristocracy who had gone to England to escape the Revolution. Mme de Gramont d'Aster had opened a school in London; now back in France, she placed her daughters, Eugénie and Antoinette, in the boarding school in Amiens. They moved in time from student status to that of novices. Their mother, also Eugénie, became a good friend of Sophie Barat and entered the Society herself. In the future, young Eugénie, the daughter, would be both a close friend and associate of Sophie, as well as the source of some of her greatest trials.

Sophie found the responsibility of superior onerous. She had to give attention to the education in the boarding school and in the free school the sisters soon opened, as well as to the material needs of the house. She soon became ill. Although she resisted being cared for, she was sent for treatment to Paris to a hospital of the Sisters of Charity, where she spent several months. We shall see that she suffered all her life from different illnesses that required bed rest, but in spite of them she maintained a demanding schedule of work.

Church law required that communities of women religious have a churchman as what was called an ecclesiastical superior who acted as a representative of the bishop in their regard. Father Varin was the ecclesiastical superior of the women as well as superior of the French branch of Fathers of the Faith. This branch separated from the Roman Fathers of the Faith because of the scandalous behavior of the Roman founder. Father Varin then informed Sophie and the sisters in Amiens that they would no longer be connected with the *Dilette* but would be an independent society called Ladies (Sisters) of Christian Instruction, a title that expressed their purpose. The name of Society of the Sacred Heart would be adopted later when it became politically safe to do so. It will be remembered that the symbol of the Sacred Heart was used by adherents of the Bourbon dynasty who opposed the Revolution.

Father Varin exercised close supervision of the community in Amiens at the beginning; it appears that he was not sure about Sophie's ability to manage. Gradually, Sophie began to take charge, but he advised especially on accepting candidates. On one occasion, he insisted that Sophie accept a young woman whose ability to teach Sophie doubted. Her response was, "Very well Father; since we are nine we need a zero to make ten." She said she got a good scolding and the postulant as a penance, but the young woman soon left, as she had no vocation.

As Father Varin was responsible for both the men and the women, he traveled a great deal and could not act as regular chaplain to the school and community in Amiens. He secured the services of another priest of the Fathers of the Faith, Louis Sambucy de Saint-Estève. He had had some experience as a tutor, and he gradually assumed a more extensive role in the school than simply that of chaplain; Anne Baudemont became his ally. This alliance was strengthened when Baudemont became acting superior in Amiens in 1804. In that year, Father Varin sent Sophie with two companions to Grenoble to meet Philippine Duchesne, a former novice in the order of the Visitation, and unite her little group of companions and their boarding school with the Amiens group.

5

THE SOCIETY FORMS

MADELEINE SOPHIE STAYED at Sainte-Marie d'En-Haut, the former Visitation monastery in Grenoble, over a year, gradually altering the way of life of Philippine and her companions, who had been formed in the classical cloistered life of women religious before the Revolution. Philippine had been a novice for four years; she had lived behind grilles; she had expected to spend the rest of her life in her monastery of the order of the Visitation. When the Revolutionary government had put an end to that hope, she returned home; but as soon as Napoleon came into power and began to restore some civic order, she succeeded through the influence of some powerful friends and relatives in obtaining possession of her monastery with a view to reviving Visitation life. Although some of the nuns returned to take up their former life, the attempt to reestablish the Visitation in Grenoble failed. When Sophie arrived, she found not only a small community and a group of students; she found a whole monastery that became the second house of the nascent Society of the Sacred Heart. And she found in Philippine a religious who would become one of her

Sainte Marie d'En-Haut

most trusted and significant associates and who would take the Society of the Sacred Heart to the New World.

After a year or so, Sophie was called elsewhere. There were two sisters in Poitiers who were running a small boarding school in a former monastery of a branch of the Cistercians called *Les Feuillants*. With a companion, Henriette Girard, Sophie went to see them and decided that this place had possibilities. She accepted one of the sisters and a companion into the Society and took over the responsibility of the boarding school. At the same time, there was a group of women in Bordeaux who wanted to lead religious life. They had formed the novel idea of leaving their family homes and moving into a kind of cabin outside of the city. Sophie interviewed them one by one, chose several and took them to Poitiers where she established the first real novitiate of the Society.

She was able to form these women to prayer and the apostolate in the spirit of dedication to the Heart of Jesus, the initial inspiration of the Society.

The Society Forms | 19

Chapel in the Novitiate

Sophie has left us the journal she kept of this first novitiate. We can imagine her, a slim, tiny young woman with brown hair and brown eyes and a penetrating gaze. She describes their life together and the teaching she imparted to them. Although she had such limited experience of religious life, here as in Grenoble, she knew what she wanted to hand on to them. She had "caught" so to speak Father de Tournély's inspiration of dedication to the glory of the Heart of Jesus, and that was to be the basis of their life together. She had the help of several priests who gave instructions, but Sophie herself spoke to them regularly on the virtues, especially humility, charity, and total dedication to the interests of the Heart of Jesus required by the life they had chosen.

Her talks on the virtues repeat commonly held views on religious life, but she shows some originality when speaking about the educational apostolate. In these conferences, she articulates her own developing philosophy of education. She is clear that the purpose of the teaching in the schools is a religious one: to inculcate good habits and devotion in order to save the souls of the children, but she is equally insistent that the curriculum must be pleasant and interesting if it is to be effective. Teachers must be "amiable," must meet the children at their level without losing dignity or compromising authority. Sophie admits that this ability is a particular gift of God for which one must pray, but it is meant to characterize teachers in schools of the Sacred Heart. Later she will stress that the teachers must be mothers to the children who are to feel that they are part of a family. At the same time, all her life she would emphasize serious study in view of intellectual development. She would write that the Society needed holy, learned women (*saintes savantes*). Some of the recipients of this teaching in the novitiate of Poitiers became Sophie's closest allies, especially Thérèse Maillucheau and Joséphine Bigeu.

As well as summarizing her teaching in the journal, Sophie portrays the role community life played in the formation of the novices. Besides study and hard work, the novices enjoyed being together, prayer together, singing and conversing. They loved Sophie, and she tells somewhat amusingly that her absences or times of retreat caused them sorrow; they missed her, and her returns were celebrated exuberantly. She bemoans the fact that her efforts to teach them detachment were in vain; their attachment to her indicates her charm, her personal magnetism. It is clear that she has great affection for them as well. She reveals also a certain intuitive awareness of each one's need for balance: for example, Thérèse Maillucheau would have loved to do nothing but pray; Sophie gave her charge of the cow. If she thought that one of them was too dependent on herself, Sophie limited her contacts; but when one of them really needed guidance and support, she was given as much time as she asked for. In these decisions, Sophie, who was no older than many others of the group, gave evidence of the wisdom and knowledge of human nature that would characterize her leadership in the future.

All was not smooth sailing, however. Clergy in general and the vicars general—the bishop was frequently absent—in Poitiers in particular were not sure about this new way of religious life for women. Specifically, they did not see how they could exercise their jurisdiction over a society whose superior moved around and had jurisdiction over houses in different dioceses. Besides, who would be *her* superior? They were used to the pre-Revolutionary style of women's religious life in which nuns lived in an independent, enclosed monastery under the local bishop. From the beginning, however, the plan, influenced by several priests, would-be Jesuits, had been that the Society would have central government resembling that of the Jesuits; there would be a superior with authority over all the houses and the possibility of moving the members from one house to another according to the needs of the schools they were to operate. It would take time and considerable negotiation to have the Society's way of life accepted.

6

DIVERGENCE

MEANWHILE THE COMMUNITY in Amiens was moving in a different direction. The acting superior in Sophie's absence, Anne Baudemont, had been formed in the monastic style just described. Her advisor, Saint-Estève, operated on the same model of a monastery of women who belonged to one house under the authority of the local bishop with only a relationship of charity with sister houses. The superior had authority over her own house only. During the years when Sophie had been away, first at Grenoble then at Poitiers, Anne Baudemont, under the influence of Saint-Estève, had gained considerable influence over the Amiens community. Most of the community favored her government, especially Saint-Estève's sister, Félicité Sambucy, and the two younger de Gramonts. Sophie's authority was challenged, and the unity of the whole was threatened. It was clear, however, that outside of Amiens, Madeleine Sophie Barat was in fact acting as the overall head of the Society. She moved from one city to another, establishing communities, accepting candidates, creating a novitiate for their formation. By

1806, with houses in Grenoble, Poitiers, in the city of Belley, as well as in Amiens, a formal gathering for the election of a superior general was held in Amiens. Professed nuns from each of the other houses were invited to send their votes. On January 18, 1806, Sophie was elected by a majority of just one vote. The other contender was Anne Baudemont, the acting superior at Amiens. The outcome did not put to rest the opposition to Sophie among the religious in Amiens. What did the others see in her? Like Louise Naudet who had named Sophie local superior four years earlier, the sisters from the other houses saw her leadership ability and, even more important, her clarity and commitment regarding the vision of dedication to the Sacred Heart of Jesus handed down by Léonor de Tournély through Joseph Varin.

It was evident that there had to be a written rule that all the houses would observe. Saint-Estève had undertaken to compose a rule with Father Varin's approval. At first, Father Varin did not see that, with Sophie's absence and his own increasing distance because of political troubles, the initial inspiration of dedication to the Sacred Heart of Jesus was gradually being lost in Amiens. Saint-Estève was not heir to Léonor de Tournély's vision as Father Varin was. Neither did he have the same understanding as Sophie had of central government. He was influenced by earlier concepts of female religious life experienced by Anne Baudemont and the other former nuns who had joined the Amiens community.

Sophie undertook to propose Saint-Estève's rule to the other houses in an effort to preserve unity. These communities did not find the spirit of the Sacred Heart in his work and did not accept it. One community whose opposition was particularly strong was in Ghent. While Sophie was away, Saint-Estève—without consulting her—had arranged for a foundation in Ghent, then in northern France. It actually took place in 1808, by eight members of the Amiens community led by Antoinette de Peñaranda, a Belgian of Spanish origin. They opened a boarding school and a free school in the former Cistercian monastery of Doorseele. By 1814, Ghent in Belgium was no longer part of France but belonged to the Netherlands. The bishop urged the community to separate from the Association of Christian Instruction. The community decided to do so, not only for political reasons but also because they were not in sympathy with the rule Saint-Estève had composed, even when Sophie visited them to present it. All the French members of the community and one of the Belgians returned to Amiens, and in December 1814, Ghent separated from the association. Sophie's stress caused by this event and the conflict over the rule resulted in her becoming seriously ill with a sinus infection that lasted three weeks. She was in danger of death and received the last sacraments. Although she had been ill several times between 1806 when she had had to be hospitalized and 1814, this last illness was the most serious. Afterward she was very weak well into spring of 1815.

Negotiations concerning the rule had to continue, nevertheless. Just at this time, Saint-Estève was imprisoned in Paris, apparently for some political activity in the diocese of Amiens. Sophie even went to Paris to discuss the question of the rule, to no effect. Once released from prison, he obtained a position in the embassy of France to the Holy See. From Rome Saint-Estève communicated that his rule was approved by the pope and that the Sacred Heart communities had to accept it. He opened a house of the association in Rome and invited his followers in Amiens to join it. His sister Félicité Sambucy and Teresa Copina, another of his followers, left Amiens for Rome without telling anyone else in the community, except Eugénie de Gramont who was wavering in her sympathies. He even went so far as to invent a Vatican official in whose name, "Stephanelli," he wrote, claiming that the pope had approved his rule and the house of the association he had founded in Rome. The deception was uncovered, and Sophie and Father Varin realized that it was necessary to start over with the composition of a rule.

7

A NEW START

IN 1814, POPE PIUS VII had restored the Society of Jesus in Europe, and the former Fathers of the Faith in France, Joseph Varin and Louis Barat among others, hastened to join it. Even though Varin was a novice, the new provincial superior, Father de Clorivière, allowed him to work with Sophie on the rule. With the aid of another Jesuit, Julien Druilhet, as draftsman, a rule was completed; and in the fall of 1815, Sophie convened a council in Paris to present it to representatives of all the houses. They approved the rule, adopted the name of Society of the Sacred Heart, established the government and regulated many details of life in the Society. Unity was preserved and the identity of the Society was firmly established.

It was decided that a house in Paris was needed as headquarters for the superior general and the location of a central novitiate as well as a Paris boarding school. A house was rented in the rue des Postes, and Philippine Duchesne, who had been elected secretary general, was put in charge of setting up the house.

Philippine had come from Grenoble for the council; she was never to return there. She had long had missionary yearnings, especially a desire to go to North America to bring the Gospel to Native Americans. Many years later, Sophie would tell the story of how these yearnings developed. She related that she herself admired Saint Francis Xavier and longed to imitate his apostolate in foreign missions; but having been assured that she was meant for France, she hoped that she would find "a soul who would sacrifice herself for the foreign missions." She confided this hope to Philippine who said nothing at the time; but later at their regular monthly talk Philippine told Sophie that she believed "she was that soul." The years passed, years when the Society was growing into its identity.

Two years after the council of 1815, Bishop Dubourg of Louisiana—then the whole territory of the Louisiana Purchase—came to the motherhouse in Paris. Encouraged by Louis Barat whom he had met in Bordeaux, he asked Mother Barat for nuns for his vast diocese. Up to that point there was a convent of Ursuline nuns in New Orleans but no other religious women in the diocese. The Society was still so small that it seemed imprudent if not impossible to accede to his request; but at Philippine Duchesne's strong urging, Sophie decided to send a group of five with Mother Duchesne at their head. Foreseeing the difficulty of communication, Sophie granted Philippine extraordinary authority, for example, to establish houses and to accept candidates. The little band set out across the Atlantic on March 21, 1818, and reached New Orleans on May 29, after a harrowing voyage, the story of which is told in Mother Duchesne's biography. This step foreshadowed the eventual development of the Society of the Sacred Heart as an international congregation that would be established in all five continents.

8

GROWTH IN FRANCE

MEANWHILE GROWTH CONTINUED in France. It soon became apparent that the small house in the rue des Postes was inadequate for the boarding school, the novitiate and the superior general's headquarters. Sophie began to search for a larger property, and just then the Hôtel Biron in the rue de Varenne, a large estate in the Faubourg Saint-Germain, was put on the market. The price was beyond the means of the Society, and besides the location risked identifying the Society with the aristocracy who lived in that part of the city. In the end, thanks to wealthy friends and a gift from the king, Sophie was able to buy the Hôtel Biron and move the boarding school there. The novitiate and the community living quarters occupied the former stables and the other outbuildings. Even so, the location of the establishment earned the Society a reputation of wealth and privilege. It was true that many of the pupils and some of the novices were from aristocratic families. Sophie formed friendships with some women of the nobility, but she always called attention to her own origins. It is told that once

Hotel Biron

some little girls refused to be taught by a sister whose name indicated that she was not an aristocrat. Hearing of it, Sophie assembled the children and said that she would have to leave them because her father was a simple working man. Regret and repentance followed.

In the same year, 1820, Sophie convened another general council to take stock of the Society's development and especially to give attention to the education in the boarding schools. A plan of study had been composed in Amiens as early as 1804, but experience there and in the other houses had shown the need of attention to the direction of the schools. Variations in curriculum and methodology had crept in, and Sophie realized that some uniformity was necessary in order to maintain a high standard. During this council a thorough revision of the plan of study was made with the guidance of Nicholas Loriquet, SJ, who had assisted Sophie and her first companions in Amiens. Concern for educational excellence was a theme from the beginning.

Father Varin gave a retreat to the members of the council during which he warned them about the dangers of association with the wealthy. He composed a treatise on the five virtues that should characterize RSCJ: faith; contempt of the world, that is of worldly standards of success; humility, modesty, and simplicity. This treatise was incorporated into the Summary of the Constitutions, which was henceforth to be read monthly in every house. The religious were to be reminded regularly of the necessity of vigilance lest religious spirit be compromised by the contacts with people of wealth that their educational work required.

Aloysia Jouve, RSCJ, wearing the original costume of the Society

In 1821, the year following the council, Sophie learned of the death in Grenoble of a young religious, Aloysia Jouve, Philippine's niece. She had been a pupil of Sainte-Marie whom both Philippine and Sophie had followed attentively as her religious vocation developed.

She showed great promise both as a religious and as a teacher when she entered the noviciate at Sainte-Marie just before Philippine left for Paris and the council of 1815. They were never to see each other again. Philippine left for America from Paris without returning to Grenoble. Aloysia was not sent to the newly established Paris noviciate as she had duties in the school at Sainte-Marie. The illness that would take her life began shortly after her first vows; it showed itself in increasingly severe wounds. Sophie hoped for a miraculous cure, and as a kind of effort to force God's hand—so to speak—she gave Aloysia several heavy responsibilities, which she fulfilled heroically. Her death, however, occurred on January 21, 1821; she was not yet twenty-five years old but already mature and full of religious virtue. Sophie is quoted as having said, "Thus I had dreamed they would all be."

9

FURTHER EXPANSION

IN THE ENSUING YEARS foundations continued as bishops asked for nuns to open schools in their dioceses. Individuals also requested boarding schools. Some properties were donated, but some had to be purchased, causing Sophie to dread accumulating debts, a fear she had her whole life. Sophie was able to answer these appeals as numbers of members increased. Individuals entered the Society, and at the same time, some small groups—like the one in Grenoble—that had not been able to reconstitute themselves after the Revolution asked to join the Society. This happened in several places and resulted in the increase in numbers.

Expansion meant an increase of work for Sophie as she had to keep an eye on how the houses were governed. It happened that some superiors were not skilled in financial administration and were too generous with financial aid or let debts accumulate. Such was the case in Grenoble where Sophie's good friend, Thérèse Mailluncheau, had let things get out of hand to the point that the house was threatened with bankruptcy. Sophie sent Thérèse to

Quimper, a smaller house, and moved to Grenoble herself. Worn out with the labor of rescuing the situation, she became seriously ill with a pernicious fever that threatened her life once again. As the news became known in all the houses, one of her nieces, Dosithée Dusaussoy, a student in Amiens, decided to offer her life to God for Sophie's cure. She soon developed a severe fever and on May 4, 1823, she died. On that same May 4, the physician who was caring for Sophie wrote to his colleague in Amiens that "after forty-five days of illness and several crises that did not peak, Mme Barat is now convalescing…." Susceptibility to such infections would haunt Sophie all her life. Almost every winter, she had to spend several weeks in bed or confined to her room with a series of illnesses; she had rheumatism, fever, digestive upsets, and consistently what she called catarrh—respiratory infection. Besides, over time she sustained several injuries, once to her right arm, then to her finger, which interfered with writing. She comments on all these, but at the same time she writes to Eugénie de Gramont in 1817, "I have very good health; I can fight illnesses…I may live to be 80." As we shall see, she was right.

Dosithée's impulse to offer her life to save Sophie's suggests that a close relationship existed between Sophie and her nieces. In fact, in spite of the multiple contacts her role demanded, Sophie did maintain an affectionate and practical relationship with her family. She was full of concern for her sister, Marie-Louise, and her children, giving each of the girls a place in one of the boarding schools. She followed up their progress in studies and conduct, giving them and their teachers useful advice about their upbringing. Their father died at the age of fifty-five, leaving Marie-Louise without many resources, so she needed Sophie's help in educating her girls, and Louis helped with the boys. Sophie too was close to her nephews; one of them recalled in later life how much he loved her when he was a little fellow and she used to take him for walks by the river. In the early days of the Society before the rules were fully developed and enforced, Sophie stopped in Joigny to spend time with her family in the course of her many journeys. She knew the younger generation well as a result.

10

PAPAL APPROBATION

AS THE SOCIETY SPREAD to more dioceses, it became increasingly obvious that to maintain unity and to safeguard the Society's way of life and apostolate, it would be necessary to have papal approval of the Constitutions and Rules. If the Constitutions were approved by Rome, local bishops could not change them or require communities to change them. Besides, Sophie wanted the religious of the Society to make solemn vows, that is, irrevocable public vows, because for her solemn vows represented an absolute form of self-giving to God. The obstacle—besides the fact that solemn vows were against the civil law in France—was that canon law required women with solemn vows to be cloistered, confined to one house. Sophie wanted, as we have seen, the possibility of personnel being moved from one house to another in function of apostolic need. She had already acted on this principle by transferring superiors here and there, and she had sent five people across the ocean. There was no question of cloister as understood in canon law. Sophie sent her close associate, Mother Joséphine Bigeu, to Rome to engage in a lengthy process of consultation with priest friends, especially one Jean Rozaven, SJ, and to negotiate with Vatican authorities. The result was a decree of approbation by Pope Leo XII, issued on December 22, 1826. To secure this approbation, Sophie had had to give up the idea of solemn vows as such, but the religious were to make at final profession a vow of stability along with the three vows of poverty, chastity, and obedience. This vow was understood as stability in the Society, replacing to some degree the vow of stability to her own monastery made by a cloistered nun. It meant that the final commitment of a religious of the Sacred Heart could be dispensed only by the pope, since it was made in the context of constitutions formally approved by the pope. Subsequently, rules concerning travel and leaving the house became more stringent, and the way of life of RSCJ came to be called "semi-cloistered."

Another significant result of the approbation process was that the pope appointed a Roman cardinal as "protector." The Society was to be subject to him instead of to the different bishops in the dioceses where convents were established. This provision further safeguarded uniformity in customs by making sure that local bishops would not be allowed to interfere with the Society's way of life. This arrangement, by which certain orders called "exempt" were not under the control of the local bishop, was relatively new for women's congregations.

In 1828, Pope Leo XII offered the monastery and church of the Trinità dei Monti on the Pincian Hill in Rome to the Society for a school for the daughters of the papal nobility. Sophie sent a trusted religious, Armande de Causans, to take charge. The Trinità was on French property, and the government required that the convent and school be staffed by French religious; but Sophie saw that Italian families, noble or not, would want an Italian education,

Trinità

and for that Italian nuns would be needed. Besides, an apostolate with children of poor families would be impossible without Italian religious. In view of providing for this need, Sophie decided she had to go to Rome. But before she could carry out this plan, there were other matters to attend to.

One day in May 1829, while still in Paris, she climbed onto a table to close a window and fell from it injuring her foot badly. It did not heal, and she could not walk, even on crutches at first. A basket on wheels was devised so that she could be wheeled about the house and garden. She wrote that sometimes the person who was to move her would forget, and she would be left in the chapel or at the top of the stairs, when the sister who was caring for her went to find someone to help lift her down the stairs. Many treatments were tried, even the baths near Chambéry, where the Society had a house, but there was no result. After some time, she was able to walk on crutches, but getting around was still difficult. This situation lasted for about three years.

11

POLITICAL TROUBLES

AT THE SAME TIME, political troubles in France were causing anxiety. One symptom was the growing demand in both chambers of the government for the banning of the Jesuits from educational work. In 1828, their eight schools were suppressed. Because the Society was closely allied with the Society of Jesus, Sophie feared that the same fate could befall her schools. The Bourbon king, Charles X, who had come to the throne in 1824, had led the country further in the direction of counter-revolutionary policies. The resulting erosion of liberties provoked the Revolution of 1830, also known as the July Revolution. It resulted in the overthrow of King Charles X and the ascent of his cousin, Louis Philippe, Duke of Orléans, who himself, after eighteen precarious years on the throne, would be overthrown in 1848. It marked the shift from one constitutional monarchy, under the restored House of Bourbon, to another under its younger branch, House of Orléans; and the replacement of the principle of hereditary right by that of popular sovereignty. Sophie realized that this development could have repercussions on the work of the Society. The Paris house, the Hôtel Biron in the rue de Varenne, was located in the heart of the Faubourg Saint-Germain, where the Bourbon-related royalists were congregated and where opposition to the new king was centered. The house was identified with them and their cause, as we have seen. As violence threatened and parents began to withdraw their children from the school, Sophie decided to leave Paris and take refuge in Conflans, just outside of Paris, where Eugénie de Gramont, superior at the Hôtel Biron, was convalescing from an illness in a small house belonging to Archbishop de Quelen of Paris. Their stay there was fraught with difficulty; the house was in the path of mobs, so they had to look for new lodging. When it was time to return to Paris, transportation was a problem. Sophie and her companions had to walk through torn up streets, and Sophie was still walking with crutches. At one point, they encountered a gentleman who was a little the worse for celebrating the revolution. He offered to carry Sophie over some rough spots, and she allowed him to do so. Once back in Paris, Sophie realized that the city was still too unsettled for safety for the students and the novices. During her absence, insurgents had entered the gardens of the Hôtel Biron, and there had been gunfire. She decided to leave Paris until calm returned. She sent the fifty novices to other houses in the south.

What to do about the students? A royalist of Sophie's acquaintance, the Marquis de Nicolay, whose daughters were pupils at the rue de Varenne, decided to send his children to Switzerland and offered Sophie hospitality in his house at Givisiers near Fribourg in that country. In August 1830, following the July days, Sophie and Eugénie de Gramont left the Hôtel Biron for Givisiers, where they stayed with the Nicolay family while looking for a suitable house for the novices and for students whose parents wanted them to remain at school at the Sacred Heart. They rented a chateau at Middes to use until the one purchased at Montet would be ready for occupancy. Novices and students were collected at Middes. In the meantime, Sophie set out for Chambéry in winter 1831. During her journey she had another accident when someone inadvertently pulled a chair she was leaning on out from under her. In April, she went with a sister companion to Aix-les-Bains in the hope of cure from the waters. Improvement allowed her to travel to Grenoble. She returned to Switzerland in time to settle novices and students in the newly renovated house at Montet, then made her way back to Paris.

During one of the outbreaks of violence in Paris, the palace of Archbishop Hyacinthe-Louis de Quelen, an ardent royalist, had been sacked. When calm returned and occupation of the Hôtel Biron again became possible, Eugénie de Gramont, superior, offered the archbishop hospitality at the Hôtel Biron. Sophie opposed this move, but the offer had been made; and with his staff, he occupied a small house on the property. Although he did not live in the convent itself, his closeness to both school and convent came to be a source of gossip and compromised the convent with people who did not sympathize with the royalists. For the next nine years, many of Sophie's letters refer to the scandal caused by the archbishop's presence at the Hôtel Biron. This situation added to her anxiety about this house.

Sophie herself did not remain in Paris but set out to visit her houses in the south on her way to Rome. Delays caused by political disturbances prevented travel for a time, and Sophie stayed in Lyon where a house had been opened in the rue Boissac. The superior, Edmée Lhuiller, a niece of Father Julien Druilhet, had begun to gather a group of alumnae and other women of the city. It was a work in progress, which Sophie saw as having great possibilities. She asked Father Druilhet to draw up rules for what was to become the Children of Mary, a religious association called a sodality that ultimately would be established in all houses of the Sacred Heart. Her prolonged stay in Lyon allowed her to oversee the development of this work.

Moving on, she went in 1832 to Avignon where she learned to her great distress that cholera had reached Paris. During this epidemic the prime minister, Casimir Perier, Philippine's cousin, was attacked by the disease when visiting a hospital where there were cholera victims; he died six weeks later. Sophie wrote to Philippine, "He was our hope."

During these days, Archbishop de Quelen visited the parts of the city where the cholera was most virulent and took all kinds of measures to aid the victims and their families. He wrote to his priests, "I know no other politics than those of St. Vincent de Paul. Like him, I am for God and the poor." His words and actions inspired Sophie, and she suggested to Eugénie de Gramont that she take in at the rue de Varenne twelve to fifteen little orphans of the cholera. It was no sooner said than done.

12

ITALY AND FURTHER EXPANSION

SOPHIE CONTINUED her journeys in the south of France and made her way into Italy where she stopped at Turin. She was still suffering from the difficulty in walking caused by the fall three years earlier. Various treatments had been tried to no avail until one skillful doctor in Turin was consulted. He saw that two bones in her foot were dislocated and promptly snapped them into place, making it possible for her to walk again.

She continued to make her way to Rome where for the first time she met Pope Gregory XVI, who had succeeded Leo XII. He would be a great friend, even champion. He had been a Camaldolese monk and is quoted as saying that his monastic education would have made him disapprove of many things about the Society of the Sacred Heart, "but its Rule is the work of God, and I would not change a word of it. The finger of God is there." Sophie's primary purpose in going to Rome was to open a Roman novitiate. She had learned that Gregory XVI wanted the Society to have an Italian novitiate to train religious for apostolic work with Roman children, especially the poor children of the

Trastevere. For them Italian-speaking teachers were needed. The pope offered her a former monastery in the Trastevere, Santa Rufina, and Sophie was able to purchase the Villa Lante on the Janiculum for the purpose of the novitiate. There were already a few novices at the Trinità, but as it was a French-speaking house, they were not learning Italian; they were brought over to inaugurate the Roman novitiate. Funds were needed for this new house, which were largely supplied by a generous noblewoman, the Marchesa Andosilla.

In 1833, Sophie was back in Paris where she held the fifth general congregation, overdue by now. The members were chiefly concerned with updating the plan of studies, again assisted by Father Loriquet, who had given such help to the Amiens community in drafting the original plan of studies and to the council of 1820. In writing to the Society after the council, Sophie urged her religious "to put more zeal into their own personal instruction and formation to study," and she asserted that improvements in the Plan would have no effect unless each one took her own responsibility for self-development. At the same time, she emphasized that in assigning duties superiors had to make sure the sisters had the time needed for study.

Regarding religious life, there was a call to stricter rules of poverty and cloister. In order to achieve greater uniformity of life style a *coutumier* or book of customs was planned, based on that of the Society of Jesus. Jesuit influence was seen also in the formal adoption of Saint Ignatius's methods of meditation. Jesuits or would-be Jesuits had been spiritual guides for the religious of the Sacred Heart from the beginning, but until now the use of Ignatian methods of prayer had not been prescribed. It is clear that Sophie interpreted this prescription widely; she wrote to one person, "It does not matter how you pray.…" Her concern was that each person follow the inspiration of the Holy Spirit.

Among other actions, a decision had to be made to close the convent and school of Sainte-Marie d'En Haut in Grenoble, for the city revoked the right to occupy it, which had been granted officially to Philippine Duchesne in 1805. Writing to Philippine, Sophie expressed her sorrow at the loss of a place so dear to both of them.

Eugénie Audé, one of Philippine's first companions, had been called from America. She was named an assistant general by this council, along with Catherine de Charbonnel, Félicité Desmarquest and Eugénie de Gramont, all three originally from Amiens. One appointment made at this council would be extremely significant for the future: that of Elisabeth Galitzine as secretary general. She was a convert to Roman Catholicism from Russian Orthodoxy who had been brought into the Church and guided to the Society by Father Rozaven, the Jesuit who had advised Joséphine Bigeu during the process of applying for papal approbation of the Constitutions. In addition, Louise de Limminghe was named adviser to the superior general. Sophie had already privately named Louise as the person to whom she would be obedient in what concerned her personal life. Her explanation was that she, Sophie, was the only one who had no one to obey, and she wanted the grace that she believed came from exercising her vow of obedience.

After the council, she traveled throughout France, ending up in Lyon where, during the winter of 1834-1835, she again became very ill. She was exhausted from travel, from the pressure of correspondence and the duties of her office. She was beginning to question her ability to continue because the number of houses and persons with whom to keep in touch was beyond her strength. The necessity of rest in Lyon gave her the opportunity to work out a plan for governing the rapidly expanding Society.

13

CRISIS

IN 1839, it was time for another General Council, the sixth. Sophie planned to hold it in Rome at the Trinità dei Monti. The main concern at this time was to provide a change in the governmental structure of the Society. It had grown rapidly and widely: from the original house in Amiens in 1801 to thirty-eight houses in 1839. One person, Sophie as superior general, could not effectively oversee all the houses and their works and remain in contact with all the members. During the years preceding, she had been working with Louise de Limminghe and Elisabeth Galitzine, advised by Father Rozaven, on some governmental changes that she believed were necessary. In addition, some improvement was needed in formation, especially regarding that of the coadjutrix sisters. The council opened on June 10, 1839, at the Trinità. Sophie was disappointed that Eugénie de Gramont, superior in Paris, was not present; she claimed that Archbishop de Quelen had forbidden her to leave. Geneviève Deshayes and Henriette Grosier, her earliest companions, were unable to come on account of age and frail health.

The group that gathered was quite small, therefore, and dominated by Mothers de Limminghe and Galitzine and influenced by Father Rozaven. The council decided on numerous changes to the Constitutions to propose to the Vatican. Among them was the organization of the houses into provinces (geographical regions) with provincial superiors, resembling the structure of the Society of Jesus. These provincial superiors would visit the houses in their province and follow the progress of the works and the members. There were also to be changes in the length of time before final profession, and the coadjutrix sisters were no longer to make the vow of stability. The most controversial decision, however, was the plan to move the residence of the superior general to Rome. Those most strongly in favor of the move, the allies of Mothers Galitzine and de Limminghe, saw opposition to the move as an example of "Gallicanism," a symptom of disloyalty to the pope. There was strong disapproval of moving the motherhouse to Rome within the Society, mainly in France, led by Eugénie de Gramont, and on the part of several French bishops who had houses of the Society in their dioceses. To allow the controversy to settle down, Sophie proposed a three-year trial period, during which she asked each house to implement the decisions as a test. During this trial period, the motherhouse was to remain in France. At the end of the trial period, she planned to have another council to evaluate the experiment. Elisabeth Galitzine was sent to America to explain the measure to be tried. As for Eugénie de Gramont in Paris, she felt that she could not begin the trial period until she knew the wishes of the new archbishop, Archbishop de Quelen having died at the end of 1839.

When the time came to call that council three years later, Sophie decided to convene it in Lyon instead of at the motherhouse in

Paris because the strongest opposition to the changes was in Paris. By this time, there was a new archbishop in Paris. Archbishop Denis Affre insisted that Sophie had no right to decide to hold a council outside of his diocese without his permission as he was ecclesiastical superior of the Society, whose headquarters were in his diocese. The Vatican had to intervene to tell him that in fact he did not have that authority. His response was to point out that in the eyes of the French government the Society, located in France, was subject to government approval and that approval was based on the provisions of the Constitutions of 1826. If the French government were to withdraw its approval based on the changes, chiefly the removal of the superior general to Rome, the result could be the dissolution of the Society in France. Hearing of Affre's objections, the archbishop of Lyon, not wanting to oppose the archbishop of Paris, withdrew his permission for the council to meet in his diocese. The members of the council had already assembled; Sophie saw no alternative but to send them home after they all made a retreat given by Jesuit Father Barelle. Unable to resolve the problem of the disunity in the Society and the opposition on the part of some bishops, Sophie appealed for help to Césaire Mathieu, archbishop of Besançon, whom she knew well as he had been confessor at the Hotel Biron. The result was an appeal to the pope who appointed a commission of cardinals to study the matter. Their recommendation was that the changes enacted in 1839 should be annulled, that the Society return to the Constitutions approved in 1826 and that the superior general remain in Paris. There was to be another general council in 1845. Elisabeth Galitzine, the strongest advocate of the 1839 measures was, therefore, the most disappointed. She had been sent to America after the 1839 decisions to promote their implementation. Now she asked to go back to America to communicate the papal decision, but it seems she really wanted to lay the groundwork for the issues to be brought up again at the next council. She visited some houses in Missouri and Louisiana and at St. Michael caught yellow fever and died on December 8, 1843.

14

EXPANSION: NEW LANDS

MEANWHILE, AMID all the stress of these years for Sophie, preoccupied as she was with constitutional questions, the Society continued to expand. Sophie was continuing to attend to the requests for houses of the Society. Between 1839 and 1842 new houses were opened in Alsace and Poland, several in Italy and France, in Ireland and England. Besides the ones actually opened, Sophie received requests from other countries in Europe, from Peru, India, Australia and Burma, the emperor of the last asking for nuns to teach his wives and daughters embroidery with gold thread. One new house saw the Society established on the continent of Africa in Algiers, the colony under French rule. In 1842, Bishop Antoine Dupuch asked for a group of RSCJ to open a school. Sophie sent six. They were installed in the former residence of the pasha, a sumptuous palace, of which Sophie would not have approved, had she seen it.

In 1841, Mother Galitzine, on her first visit to North America was instrumental in launching several foundations. She arranged for a group to go to Saint-Jacques de l'Achigan, near Montreal, the first Canadian house; and she negotiated with the Jesuits the mission to Sugar Creek, Kansas, where Philippine Duchesne at last realized her dream of being with the Native Americans. Elisabeth Galitzine also undertook a foundation in New York. She rented a house in Manhattan near the cathedral to open a boarding school. Aloysia Hardey, up to that time superior at St. Michael in Louisiana, was put in charge as superior, thus beginning her long career of overseeing foundations and governing houses and the regional structures in the United States and Canada.

Two religious from Paris, Aimée d'Avenas and Elisa Croft, were sent to Ireland to meet a community of Brigittine Sisters in Roscrea who wanted to join the Society. The merger was completed, and the two RSCJ then went to England where a British aristocrat, Lord Clifford (whose daughter was in the Paris novitiate), offered the Society a property in Cannington in Dorset. There were already three sister postulants waiting for them. In the meantime, another Catholic gentleman offered another property called Berrymead Priory. As the Cannington location seemed less desirable, presented several obstacles and was slow in getting started, Berrymead was accepted. Sophie consented but against her better judgment. She soon realized the impossibility of sustaining both and decided to go to England in 1844, to assess the relative merits of the two locations. She crossed the Channel without difficulty, even though her companions were seasick. Once in England she experienced train travel for the first time, going from Berrymead to Cannington. Having visited both places, she decided to close Cannington and keep Berrymead, soon to move to Roehampton, which became the center of RSCJ life in England, with its prominent boarding school and novitiate. In the future, it would give the Society two superiors general, Mabel Digby and Janet Stuart.

Expansion: New Lands | 55

Mater Admirabilis

An interesting young woman joined the Society in 1844. She was Pauline Perdrau, an accomplished portrait painter, whose mother persuaded Sophie that her daughter should be sent to the Trinità in Rome as a postulant so she could continue to develop her artistic talent. She was studying with a group of artists who had a studio on the property of the Trinità while living in the convent with the community. One day during a community meeting the superior was called away, and Pauline was inspired to offer to paint a picture of Mary on the wall behind the superior's chair. She was given permission and began her work with the advice of an instructor, as she was not experienced in fresco painting. When it was finished, the fresco's colors were so garish that the superior covered it with a drape. Sometime later as the fresco dried, the colors took on a pleasing tone. The painting was uncovered, revealing the pink clad figure of the young Mary in the Temple before the Angel's message came to her. Pope Pius IX himself, among others, named it *Mater Admirabilis*. Sophie admired it, saying to Pauline, "I quite like your little Madonna." Mary was the age of the children whose education was Sophie's life work.

Sophie spent the winter of 1844-1845 in Rome. It was a severe winter, and Sophie fell ill again and had to stay in bed for several weeks. The stress of the last several years had its effect on her health, and for the rest of her life she was ill for a long time almost every winter. She confided to Archbishop Mathieu that she was "getting old. The slightest fatigue gives me endless maladies."

In June 1845, Sophie began the journey back to France, stopping at several of the houses in Italy. When she reached Turin, she learned that Louis Barat had died. He had been suffering a great deal at the end. Sophie asked for a day of solitude to mourn.

15

INTERNAL CHALLENGE

ONCE BACK IN PARIS, one of her concerns, in fact the major one, was to resolve the problem surrounding the Hôtel Biron, rue de Varenne, the center of opposition to the 1839 decrees. The superior there, Eugénie de Gramont, to whom Sophie had been close from Amiens days, had been one of the followers of Saint-Estève, but unlike some of the others, she had remained in the Society and loyal to Sophie. She had been given responsible positions from the beginning, as she was very capable. She was an attractive, winning personality, in spite of a physical handicap. As superior, she had made the Hôtel Biron what one historian called a convent à *la mode*, and she herself was a person of influence in the Faubourg Saint-Germain, the center of those royalists, adherents of the Bourbons, who were opposed to the successive regimes after the fall of Napoleon. Archbishop de Quelen's presence on the Hôtel Biron property until his death in 1839 had further increased the school's reputation as a center of high society and its identification with the royalist cause. Friends among the clergy and the laity urged

Sophie to take steps to counteract this reputation. She herself believed the studies had to be improved and school life simplified; but she could not see adopting the solution many proposed, namely, the removal of Eugénie de Gramont. It is likely that she knew that admiration of Eugénie was such that to remove her would cause severe repercussions among the school's constituency.

Instead, Sophie decided to make a formal visit of the house herself and undertake a reform. In July 1846, she moved into the Hôtel Biron. Eugénie had become ill as a result of caring for some children during an epidemic earlier. Now her overall health was declining, and she saw that her ascendancy was coming to an end. She became ill again in the fall of 1846 and died on December 1, at the age of 57 after a full reconciliation with Sophie. She was one of the keystones of the foundation of the Society and had given her whole life to the Hôtel Biron. Sophie's relationship with her and her way of handling the problem Eugénie presented illustrates Sophie's loyalty to her friends and her way of maintaining unity. She governed through the relationships she created. All her life she surrounded herself with RSCJ to whom she gave confidence and with whom she formed friendships, even with people of different ages and different points of view.

16

FURTHER REVOLUTIONS

ESTABLISHING NEW houses and schools was one side of the coin that described the Society's history in mid-nineteenth century. On the other hand, revolutions and uprisings in several countries characterized the era. Houses had to be closed, either as safety measures when violence threatened students and religious or when unfriendly legislation decreed expulsion of religious. Sophie had to close the house she had opened in Montet in Switzerland in 1830 as a refuge for religious and novices from France. In the mid-1800s, the houses recently found in the north of Italy were all closed as the forces of Garibaldi advanced, threatening violence and destruction.

One important establishment that had to close was in Turin. Besides the fashionable boarding school for children of the nobility, Anna du Rousier, the superior, had taken over a teacher training program for young girls from rural areas to train them as elementary school teachers in their villages. Even this was given up, as the nuns had to leave for safety's sake. Mother du Rousier was the last one to leave the city and went to Paris where she was put in charge of the school at the rue de Varenne. There this highly successful educator was unsuccessful at winning over the children. Sophie later sent her to North America as visitor, then to Chile where she founded the same kind of teacher training program she had supervised in Turin.

In 1850, there occurred two significant events: the death of Father Varin and the 50th anniversary of the Society's founding. Although after the papal approval of the Society, Joseph Varin had no official role in the Society's development, he continued his interest in its history. Sometimes he did not approve of actions taken, as in 1839; he felt then that some of the decisions were not in keeping with the Society's original purpose. However, he continued to be close to the members, to visit the novices, for example, for spiritual talks; and he was the only one who with Sophie could tell the story of the earliest days. Upon his death, Sophie paid tribute to his role in the foundation and acknowledged that after God the Society owed its existence to him.

Sophie was in Rome for the 50th anniversary of the Society's founding, which was celebrated on November 21, 1850. The superior general of the Jesuits, Johann Roothaan, came to pay his respects and congratulated her on her long years of service as superior general. She is quoted as answering, "That is no credit to me; it means I have been too well taken care of." There was a prayer of thanksgiving in the afternoon at which a preacher went on too long praising the Society and especially its mother general. Sophie was seen leaving the chapel while he was still talking. Afterward, she asked Mother de Limminghe who he was and said that he was never to be invited to preach again. She could not stand that kind of fulsome praise.

17

CONSOLIDATION

THE POLITICAL INSTABILITY in Europe in the 1840s meant that for several years it was impossible for Sophie to call the general council that had been decided on after the settlement of the issue of the Constitutions following the 1839 crisis. By 1850, she believed that political conditions had improved to the point that she could convene a council. It was time to revisit the question of provinces. Since 1843, she had been availing herself of the provision in the Constitutions that allowed her to name people to help her in government in specific geographical areas without formally setting up provinces with provincial superiors. The expansion that led to the desire for provinces in the first place was still making it impossible for one person to conduct visits regularly and frequently enough to ensure unity and maintenance of high standards. Sophie decided, therefore, to petition the Holy See for an exception to the decree of 1843 allowing for the formal creation of provinces as in the Society of Jesus and many other congregations. A new pope, Pius IX, assigned the matter to a commission of cardinals who saw no reason for a change and therefore refused. Sophie was downcast because she did not see how she could continue to manage with the current structure. The pope, hearing of her disappointment, sent a cleric to find out what she wanted and why. His report caused the pope to decide that the Society could create geographic divisions; but instead of provinces, they were to be called vicariates with the superiors called vicars, thus indicating a close dependence on the central authority.

In 1851, Sophie called a general council, the primary purpose of which was to ratify the new governmental structure, which provided also for a general council consisting of the vicars instead of the council of twelve as specified in the Constitutions approved in 1826. This new plan was approved to Sophie's satisfaction because she could now hand over to the vicars the responsibility of making regular visits to the houses, assigning duties to local officers and supervising the works of the houses.

At this council, Sophie asked to be allowed to resign, but her plea was refused. She was, however, allowed to name a vicar general who would replace her upon her death and govern until a general council could elect her successor, thus providing for leadership in the interim. She chose the mistress of novices of the time, Joséphine Gœtz. She had named her successor.

Besides the fact that the reputation of the Hôtel Biron made it an unsuitable location for the motherhouse, the presence of a large school did not allow for an atmosphere conducive to the formation of novices and the probanists (religious in probation preparing for final profession) and the increasing work of the generalate. The search was on for a new, separate motherhouse. Successive buildings, either rented or purchased, proved unsuccessful for one reason or another. Sophie and the motherhouse personnel had only just moved into the last one when the city informed her that the property was to be appropriated as part of an extensive urban renewal project. With the funds realized, Sophie decided to solve the problem by building on the grounds of the Hôtel Biron. The new building was at the far end of the property from the Hôtel and faced the street at right angles to the rue de Varenne. From 1859 until her death, Sophie's address was 33 Boulevard des Invalides.

Motherhouse, 33 Bd des Invalides.
The Balcony marks Sophie's room.

| 18 |

OLD AGE

HER TRAVELING DAYS over, the aged mother general was able to lead community life in a way that earlier travel had prevented. She could give herself to prayer without the distraction and interference of complex business. She left very few notes about her own prayer. We must infer from her teaching in conferences and letters how important prayer was to her, how much she relied on the Holy Spirit. We do know that in the midst of the crisis of the 1830s and 40s, she bemoaned the loss of the prayer she once had; she attributed the loss to her infidelity, of which she was always accusing herself. Her sisters saw it differently. Several testified to the states of deep prayer they had observed. In Amiens on the morning of her first vows, she did not appear and was found under a tree in the garden, quite lost in prayer. On another occasion many years later, after assisting at a presentation in the school, she did not respond in the usual way by thanking the children; instead, she sat in silence totally recollected. Finally, the mistress general had to tell the children that Reverend Mother wished to pray about what she had just heard. The children were dismissed in silence and the room rearranged before Sophie came to herself. These occasions do not seem to have been numerous, however, and she did not encourage her sisters to look for special spiritual favors. Regarding visions, she had once written to Eugénie de Gramont, "I'll believe in visions when you have them." Both of them seemed to have had a rather grounded spirituality.

She spent her time attending to her correspondence and conferring with people who came to see her on Society business, both religious from other houses and clerics. She had the help of a competent secretary, Adèle Cahier, but she still wrote many letters herself. The local community received her attention also; she took part in the daily recreation; and we are told that some afternoons a sign would appear on the bulletin board saying that "our Mother" would meet those who were free in the orchard to pick fruit or harvest nuts. It seemed everyone managed to be free.

But the occupation that attracted her most was meeting the little girls from the Hôtel Biron. There was a wall with a green wooden door separating the motherhouse gardens from those of the school. The children and their mistress, Mother Pauline Perdrau, (the painter of *Mater Admirabilis*) used to watch the door in the afternoon. An open door meant that Mother Barat was coming to see them, and she never came empty-handed; she was known for sumptuous *goûters*, always accompanied by a little word about God.

Children were her preoccupation from the beginning. There is a quotation attributed to her over and over: "For the sake of one child, I would have founded the Society." The occasion that gave rise to this saying was this: Sophie heard about a former student of the Hôtel Biron, a Mexican, who went back to her own country

Sophie in old age at recreation.

and became an itinerant missionary, traveling on horseback to remote villages to work for religious renewal based on devotion to the Sacred Heart of Jesus. Her name was Ofelia Plise. Sophie exclaimed "For an Ofelia, I would have founded the Society." Then she immediately corrected herself: "What am I saying? Jesus Christ is the founder; but to have formed a single student of this stamp would make all our sacrifices a joy."

Sophie had one protégée quite different from Ofelia and the little girls of the junior school. Her name was Julia de

Wicka. A Russian countess living in Paris read in a newspaper about this young wanderer who spoke a strange language. The countess went to Marseille to see if she was a compatriot. She found a street urchin speaking a language no one recognized. The countess took her back to Paris to the Hôtel Biron where Julia rapidly learned French and some manners; but she proved ungrateful to her benefactor and did not profit from her education until Mother Barat took charge of her. She had Mother Perdrau give Julia painting lessons, at which the girl became quite skillful. Soon she asked for baptism and seemed determined to lead a good Christian life, but her good intentions did not last. She was given to lying, stealing, drinking, and spreading false rumors even about Sophie. Sophie would not give up on her and sent her to several different houses, even as far as Manhattanville, asking the nuns to try to reform her. Always Sophie wrote to her to encourage her; there are over 200 letters to her. In the end, Julia was converted and married a devout Christian husband who had her soul's salvation at heart. Julia died a peaceful Christian death about seven years after Sophie's, thus justifying, perhaps, Sophie's insistence on supporting her against all appearances of success.

19

LAST ACTS OF GOVERNANCE

IN 1864, SOPHIE called the last council of her long life. It was overdue, but as before, political disturbances in Europe as well as civil war in America had interfered with the possibility of travel to Paris. Chief among the items on the agenda was teacher formation. It established two juniorate programs: after first vows each religious destined for teaching was to spend several months in teacher training; a second program before probation was aimed at those whose talents indicated that they should be trained in supervision and curriculum development. Sophie had long aspired to initiate these programs; they would be implemented only by her successor. As she had earlier, she offered her resignation; again a resounding "No," but the council allowed her to make use of the assistance of her vicar general during the time she had left. Joséphine Gœtz came to live at the motherhouse and worked closely with Sophie.

Adèle Cahier, the biographer who knew Sophie best and was present for her last days described them thus: On the Sunday before Ascension Thursday in 1865, Sophie joined the community for recreation. As she entered the room, she said she was happy to be with them that day "…because on Thursday we are going to heaven." Her hearers assumed she was referring to the celebration of the feast. On Monday, she rose, prayed, went to Mass and had breakfast as usual, after which she said she did not feel well, that she had a headache. She had a stroke a few minutes later, and was unable to speak thereafter. Earlier she had said that she would not have any "last words" that people could quote. It was true, but she was conscious: her sisters asked for a blessing; she raised her hand as if to bless them, but when her doctor asked for her blessing, there was no response. Did she think she had no authority to give him a blessing? It is likely. She lingered until Thursday; and then on Ascension Day at precisely eleven o'clock at night, she left them. Everyone present was sure she had gone to heaven.

Sophie lying in state

AFTERWORD

WAS SHE SAINTLY? If our image of saintliness involves a certain sweetness, pliancy, dutifulness, charity and compassion, a high degree of prayerfulness, all those are, of course, qualities one would expect to find in a greater or lesser degree in saints. She had them in abundance. She was canonized specifically for her humility and charity. But what about ingenuity, determination, endurance, impatience, conviction, irony, wit, what the French call *malice*, as in "…a zero will make 10"? We find these in equal measure in Sophie Barat. Her education had developed in her a respect for the mind, for hard work and achievement, and these too she left as a legacy to her followers.

Why write and read saints' lives? To be challenged, to be inspired, to be called to authentic discipleship. To what does Madeleine Sophie Barat's life call us? What is the challenge of her life? Total dedication to Jesus, the One to the glory of whose heart she had committed herself; total self-giving to God in the person of those with whom she interacted, whether her sisters, the children, friends, passing acquaintances…. She valued each person:

"For the sake of an Ofelia, I would have founded the Society." She wanted each one's full intellectual development, full use of her gifts. She understood holiness in Religious of the Sacred Heart to mean becoming *saintes savantes*, learned holy persons. She said that becoming so would be the fulfillment of their vocation.

On September 8, 1865, the general council chose as superior general, Joséphine Gœtz, whose election had practically been assured when Sophie had named her as vicar general. One of her earliest actions was to commission a biography of Sophie in view of her possible canonization. Adèle Cahier, secretary general for the last twenty years of Sophie's term of office, had been preparing for this by organizing all Sophie's papers and keeping detailed records of events. She prepared a lengthy biography, but the assistants general decided that it would be better to have a biography authored by a priest. The Abbé Louis Baunard was chosen, and Mother Cahier promptly handed over to him all the work she had done. His "Life" was published commercially, appearing in 1877, but hers was subsequently published for the Society only.

As early as 1870, Pope Pius IX told Mother Gœtz that he wanted to see Sophie's cause of canonization introduced. A diocesan information process was opened in 1872 in Paris and in Rome later the same year. The next step was to collect from her correspondents all the letters still in existence; they amounted to around 14,000. The cause of canonization was introduced in the Vatican in 1879, allowing Sophie to have the title Venerable. Further steps included exhuming the body, which had been buried in a crypt in Conflans. It proved to be intact; it was reburied in a leaden casket. When it was necessary to close all the houses in France, the body was moved to Jette-Saint-Pierre near Brussels.

During the next several years, Vatican authorities examined the writings and collected eyewitness testimonies to her virtue and way of life. Finally, in 1905, Pius X pronounced her virtues "heroic." Subsequently, two miracles were verified, and on May 24, 1908, she was declared Blessed. In 1924, two more miracles were accepted, and on May 24, 1925, Madeleine Sophie Barat was canonized, that is, declared a saint, by Pope Pius XI.

In 2009, her body was moved back to France and enshrined in the church of Saint Francis Xavier in Paris, close to the house in which she died, where she is venerated today.

Casket in which Sophie's body rests.

CHRONOLOGY

1779 Birth of Madeleine Sophie Barat in Joigny
1795 Arrival in Paris
1800 First consecration to the Sacred Heart of Jesus
1801 First house of the Sacred Heart in Amiens
1804 Foundation in Grenoble; entrance of Philippine Duchesne
1806 Election of Madeleine Sophie superior general Foundation in Poitiers, first novitiate
1815 Adoption of the Constitutions and name of Society of the Sacred Heart of Jesus
1818 Mission to America
1820 Purchase of the Hôtel Biron
1826 Papal approbation of the Constitutions
1839 Sixth General Congregation: governmental crisis; threat to unity
1851 Papal approval of establishment of vicariates
1865 Death of Madeleine Sophie Barat
1908 Beatification
1925 Canonization